Bedtime Stories
for your
DOGGIE

Written By:
Herbert Kavet

Illustrated By:
Martin Riskin

© 1993
by **Ivory Tower Publishing Company, Inc.**
All Rights Reserved

Manufactured in the United States of America

30 29 28 27 26 25 24 23 22 21 20 19 18 17 16 15 14 13 12 11 10 9 8 7 6 5 4 3 2 1

Ivory Tower Publishing Co., Inc.
125 Walnut St., P.O. Box 9132, Watertown, MA 02272-9132
Telephone #: (617) 923-1111   Fax #: (617) 923-8839

Introduction

Dogs fall asleep all the time. To be honest, dogs don't need bedtime stories to fall asleep. They can even sleep while watching playoff football games on TV. It's safe to confess all this here in the Introduction. No one ever reads introductions, least of all in my books, where everyone wants to get on to Marty Riskin's cartoons. Marty is especially brilliant with dog cartoons, but he won't read this either, so I won't have to pay him extra for all his talent. Perhaps years later, when you are rereading this book for the umpteenth time, you will notice this page and give it a perusal. By then, it will be too late. The book will be long paid for and all scuffed up, and you won't be able to return it.

hy This Book Was Written

You people who remember six-page term papers from high school will recognize this page immediately for what it really is: a filler. You think it's easy coming up with 96 pages of stories that a dog, whose basic interest is only food, is actually going to sit and listen to? No way. That's also why there are a couple of blank pages at the beginning and end of this and every other book you'll ever read. Fillers. But all of this is besides the point. The purpose of this book is to help put your dog to sleep so he or she can be full of energy to demand a walk at an inconvenient time, jump up and down on you after you've gotten dressed or bowl over the kids when hearing the can of dog food being opened.

Mealtime Lament

My bowl is licked completely clean;
A single morsel can't be seen.
It's time to wait forever now,
Till once again it's time for chow.

ittle Dog Horner

Little Dog Horner
Sat in the corner,
Chewing a stick from the street.

He gnawed on the wood,
And thought it was good,
But really preferred to eat meat.

Hush-a-Bye Doggie

Hush-a-bye Doggie,
  Watch the tree top,
Pussy is up where
  You can't make her drop.

Hide 'round the corner
  So she won't fear;
When she comes down,
  You can chew on her ear.

The Three Little Piggy Dogs

The three little piggy dogs weren't called that because they were fussy eaters. Oh, no, they would eat anything in sight and their table manners weren't so great either. They were called the three little piggy dogs because all they did was think of food morning, noon and night. They were piggies all right, and their names were Royal, Kelev and Shane, and they lived with a gay couple in a condo on Commonwealth Avenue in Boston.

One day Royal awoke early and found the gay couple had already filled their three bowls with liver by-products, vegetable gums and a bunch of chemicals whose names she could not pronounce. Royal gobbled up her breakfast, nevertheless, and thinking it was yummy, proceeded to check out Kelev's bowl, just to make sure he didn't get more than her. Between checking and nibbling at Kelev's bowl, it wasn't too long before it was empty. "Uh oh," thought Royal, "Kelev will be apoplectic when he finds I've eaten his breakfast." Then she had an idea. "Why not eat Shane's bowl, too, and pretend the gay couple forgot to put out all our breakfasts?" And she did.

Kelev awoke hungry as ever and sauntered into the kitchen. You can imagine his surprise to see all their bowls empty. Finding nothing to eat and already feeling a little weak from hunger, he sauntered out the back door to check the neighbor's garbage can. This morning was good hunting because under the Colombian coffee grounds, Kelev found the remains of a roast duck dinner. Now, dogs aren't supposed to eat duck because the bones can make them choke, but Kelev never believed that old wives' tale, and he frolicked in the garbage can until all the duck was gone.

Shane awoke late and finding his bowl empty and the neighbor's garbage can picked clean, he started the day quite grumpy. Besides, the weather was humid and he was having trouble controlling the fleas. But Shane was also the cleverest of the three and before he grew any hungrier, he ran across the avenue to visit the back of an Irish pub that always had good pickings. He almost got killed crossing the street because Bostonians tend to drive like that.

The Three Little Piggy Dogs

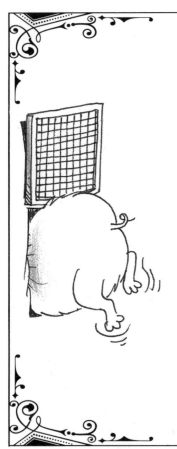

Shane had trouble getting into the bar. He huffed and he puffed, but as any idiot knows, you can't blow down brick walls, even those built under the eye of a greedy, politically-appointed building inspector who would ignore any code violation for a color TV. Finally, Shane crawled through an air vent and found himself in pig heaven. Lying on the floor among the whiskey bottles were the remains of several corned beef dinners, and he ate and ate until he could eat no more. When he was ready to leave, Shane found he could no longer squeeze through the vent. A kindly kitchen worker, who spoke no English, saw him struggling, picked him up and used him as a hood ornament on his 1968 DeSoto.

Peter, Peter, Garbage-Eater

Peter, Peter, garbage-eater,
Liked his snacks a little sweeter;
Found some yams and lobster shell,
It made his breath just smell like hell.

There Was A Crooked Dog

*T*here was a crooked dog,
   And she ran a crooked mile
To catch a tennis ball;
   This game was really vile.
Her master threw it high,
   And then he bid her fetch;
The fuzz tasted so bad
   It almost made her retch.

Hickory, Dickory, Dock

Hickory, dickory, dock,
I'll sit and watch the clock.
It's time to eat,
I want my treat,
Hickory, dickory, dock.

Hickory, dickory, dock,
Must I suck on a rock?
I need some food,
I'm in the mood,
Hickory, dickory, dock.

The Little Pup That Could

The Little Pup That Could lived in an old wooden house just a little outside of town. His days were spent in a pleasant enough yard closed in by a high, high fence. The puppy would lie in the shade and chew on a stick and do his business in a far corner, and never, ever got yelled at when poking about the yard.

But outside the yard was a wonderful forest filled with squirrels and chipmunks and birds and all sorts of things to taste and sniff. The puppy wanted to go play in this forest in the worst way. "I wonder," thought the puppy, "if I jumped really high, could I jump over the fence?" The fence stretched way up into the air and looked fearsomely high, but still the puppy wondered. Finally, he decided to try to jump over the fence, and, starting way back so as to get a good running start, ran forward, repeating to himself (since dogs can't talk), "I think I can, I think I can."

"I think I can, I think I can," he kept repeating as he leaped and jumped and struggled into the air. Finally, with one extraordinary effort, he cleared the fence and landed, a little stunned but thrilled, at the edge of the forest. "I knew I could, I knew I could," he thought happily. For the rest of the day, the puppy frolicked in the woods, getting dirty and stung and all sniffed out. When he returned for supper that night, his master was both worried and angry, and attached a stout chain from a post to the puppy's collar so he had to sit in a little corner of the yard for ever after.

The moral of this story is, if you're going to jump fences, don't come back—and be prepared to dine on squirrels and chipmunks for the rest of your life.

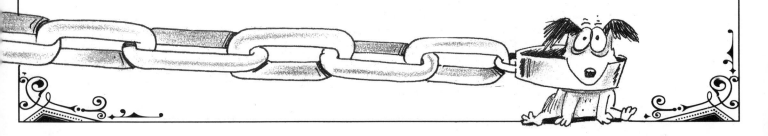

The Old Spaniel That Lived In A Shoe

There was an old Spaniel
Who lived in a shoe,
With so many puppies,
The shoe was a zoo.

Since none were yet housebroke,
It was a disgrace,
With wee wee and doo doo
All over the place.

Dog Howl

A dog named Howl would eat no fowl;
His wife thought meat obscene.
And so, betwixt them both, you see,
They licked the trash can clean.

Pat-A-Pup

Pat-a-pup, pat-a-pup,
   Give me a hug,
I hope my master
   Is getting my grub.

Rub me and scratch me
   Up safe on your lap,
After I've eaten,
   It's time for my nap.

Little Puppy

I like little puppy,
Her fur is so warm,
And if I don't hurt her,
She'll do me no harm.

But pull on her tail
Or step on a paw,
And puppy will bite you
And pee on the floor.

To Market

To market, to market,
*   To buy some dog food,*
Home again, open it,
*   I'm in the mood.*

To market, to market,
*   Let's buy some fresh duck,*
Home again, home again,
*   Bones I can suck.*

To market, to market,
*   It's liver today,*
Home again, home again,
*   Who cares what I weigh?*

The Three Silly Dogs Gruff

Once upon a time, there were three silly dogs who had to go over a little railroad bridge to get to a Chinese restaurant down near the tracks, which had the most yummy garbage cans out back. Under this bridge lived an ugly troll. Now trolls, as everyone knows nowadays, are ugly beasts imported from Taiwan with flashy neon-colored hair on top.

First to cross the bridge was the youngest silly dog. *Pit pat, pit pat* came her footsteps. "WHO'S THAT CROSSING MY BRIDGE?" roared the troll. "It's only I," said the little silly dog. "Well, I'm going to gobble you up," screamed the troll. But keeping her cool, the littlest silly dog said, "Oh, Mr. Troll, I'm much too skinny and bony for you to bother with. Why don't you wait for my fatter brother?" "Well, be off with you then," said the troll, who hated to pick too many bones out of his dinner.

A little later came the second silly dog. *Pit pat, pit pat* went his footsteps. "WHO'S THAT CROSSING MY BRIDGE?" roared the troll once again. "I'm going to gobble you up." "Oh please, Mr. Troll, you wouldn't want to gobble me up. I've been having gastric distress all week, if you get my drift. Why don't you wait for my fatter and healthier brother?" said Medium Silly Dog Gruff. "Very well, be off with you," said the troll, who had a rather sensitive stomach himself.

Then at last came MAX, the biggest silly dog. *PIT PAT, PIT PAT* went the footsteps. Then the troll popped his head over the edge and threatened to gobble up the dog, but Max didn't even hear him. Max thought the troll was a cute new doggy squeeze toy and took him home and rolled him around in the corner of the TV room for hours and chewed on his neck.

The Little Dog With The Curl

There was a little dog
Who had a little curl,
Right in the middle of his tail.

The whole house understood
He was never very good,
Especially when chewing up the mail.

uppy Dog

Puppy dog, puppy dog, run away home.
Dinner is ready, it might be a bone,
Or maybe some kidney that came from a can,
Or reprocessed pig parts diluted with bran.

Old King Tease

Old King Tease
Was a Pekingese,
And a merry old dog was he.

He drank from the john,
And when he would yawn,
Had breath that would wilt a tree.

*N*ow Old King Tease
Wanted just to please,
But his breath would make your eyes tear.

He'd come for a kiss,
Thinking nothing amiss,
But his friends would all disappear.

Green Dogs Eat Spam

Do you think green dogs eat Spam?

I do not really give a damn.

Would they eat it with a clam,
Or perhaps a bit of jam?

Would they eat it with a bone,
Or a chocolate ice cream cone?

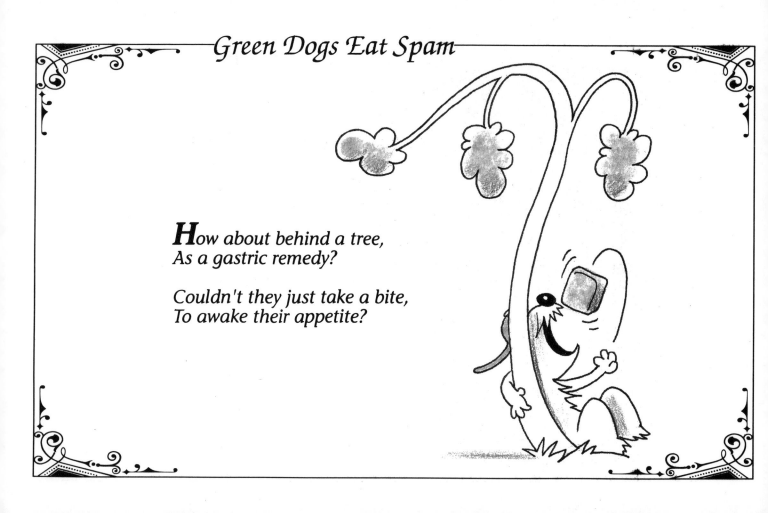

How about behind a tree,
As a gastric remedy?

Couldn't they just take a bite,
To awake their appetite?

Green Dogs Eat Spam

For all I care that dumb green thing
Can bark all night or learn to sing.

Green dogs eat Spam, or not, you see,
Is just no big concern to me.

Listen, do not be a louse;
Would they eat Spam with a mouse?

Or suppose as day began,
From a neighbor's garbage can?

Green Dogs Eat Spam

I've had enough, you make me sick,
Your head is just a bit too thick.

Just take your Spam and green dogs, too,
And let me tell you what to do.

Bend over far and touch your toe,
And I will show you where to go.

Old Mother Hubbard

Old Mother Hubbard
Went to the cupboard
To give her dog, Nudnick, a treat.

But when she got there,
The cupboard was bare,
So Nudnick just sucked on his feet.

Frisky

Frisky was a Shepherd,
  Frisky was a thief;
Frisky in the kitchen,
  Stole a piece of beef.

When I went to Frisky's place,
  Frisky was not home.
Frisky in the garbage can,
  Chewing on a bone.

Frisky

*I*thought she might be hungry,
  And dumped food in her bowl,
But when she finished dog food,
  She ate my casserole.

Now I was getting angry
  With this naughty little pet,
So just to show her who was boss,
  I fixed her at the vet.

Scott

A *retriever who answered to "SCOTT,"*
Enjoyed chasing chipmunks a lot.
He'd dig at their lair,
Would find no one there,
Then rest in his favorite spot.

isu, The Sniffer

Sisu was a sniffer. He sniffed trees and hydrants and garbage cans and other dogs of either sex, sometimes to their intense discomfort. He sniffed other dogs' bottoms and their tops and their fronts but, frankly, mostly their behinds. Sisu loved to sniff people also, and he spent a lot of time embarrassing them by sniffing their crotches.

Sisu would often lie on the cool tiles in the hallway. When he sniffed his dinner being prepared, he would bound into the kitchen and wait with almost unbearable excitement, drooling by his bowl. The smell of dinner was always a wonderful surprise to Sisu. Dinner had been happening each and every day of his life, but Sisu would forget and treat every dinner as a major celebration, equivalent, at least, to Christmas, the Fourth of July or Super Sunday. It was important to be able to sniff out such joy early.

When Sisu ate, he tended to gobble his food, which would, at times, lead to some gastric distress, if you get my meaning. When this happened, Sisu would make little emissions which he thought quite harmless, but which people found very offensive. They would all hold their noses and, fanning the air fervently, say "whew!" Sisu knew people could open doors and work cars and can openers, but he never thought human people to possess particularly sensitive olfactory nerves. This confused Sisu, and he would have liked to examine the problem further, but he was always sent from the room at times like this.

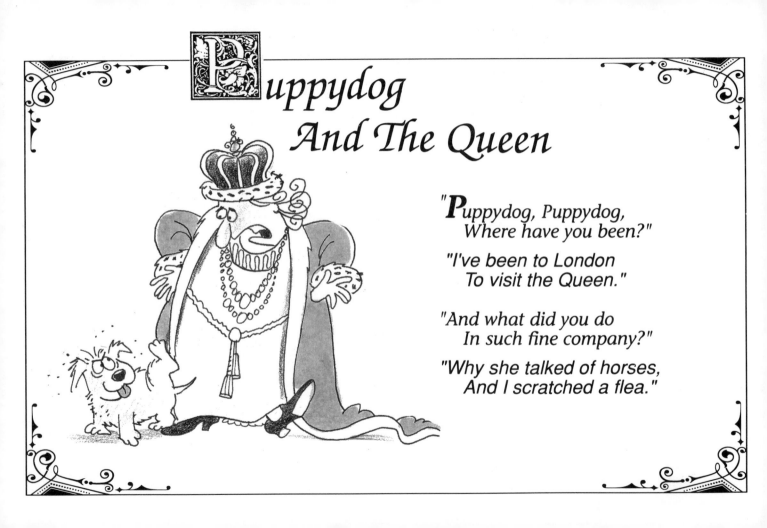

Puppydog And The Queen

"**P**uppydog, Puppydog,
     Where have you been?"

"I've been to London
     To visit the Queen."

"And what did you do
     In such fine company?"

"Why she talked of horses,
     And I scratched a flea."

Jack Be Nimble

Jack, be nimble,
  Jack, be quick,
Jack go run
  And fetch a stick.

This game is stupid,
  You'll agree,
And fills my mouth
  With wood debris.

Sing A Song Of Sixpence

Sing a song of sixpence,
  The house is full of flies.
They're pretty hard to catch
  'Cause they have ten thousand eyes.

Butterflies are playthings
  That are a lot more fun.
I catch them when they fly too low
  And eat them in the sun.

My Master's in the TV room
With a football game.
Mistress is in the kitchen
Cooking with a flame.

The kids are in the garden
In a hole they dug.
Perhaps I'll walk around in it
And track it on the rug.

Hey, Diddle, Diddle

Hey, diddle, diddle,
The dog and the fiddle,
My master's away for the day.

I'll chew on a shoe,
And drink from the loo,
And on top of white cushions will play.

Curious Georgette
Goes To The Vet

Curious Georgette was a darling old English Sheepdog who was always curious. Mostly, she was curious about male dogs and this curiosity led to four litters of puppies in the last four years. "Enough!" cried her mistress, "Enough!" cried her master. "Curious Georgette has had enough puppies. It's time to take her to the vet and get her FIXED."

Now Curious Georgette was never thrilled to go to the vet in the first place and would hide under the living room couch whenever she heard the word mentioned. Her owners used to spell it out when they talked so Georgette wouldn't understand. "I think we have to take Georgette to the V-E-T," they would say. This worked at first, but after a few months, Georgette caught on. So when Georgette heard the letters 'V-E-T,' she high-tailed it into the furthest back reaches under the living room couch and fortified herself there.

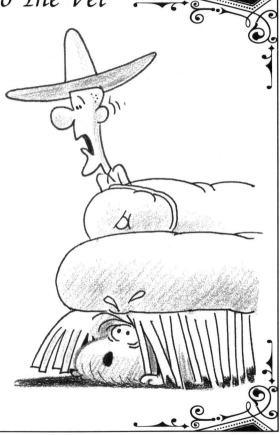

Curious Georgette Goes To The Vet

"Here, Georgie, Georgie," said her master, "here's a nice dog biscuit." "Here, Puppy, it's din-din time," said her mistress (though Curious Georgette knew it wasn't). "How about a nice can of liver parts?" "They must think I have the brains of a flea," thought Georgette. "A lousy can of artificially generated liver waste products to get me to go TO THE VET?" Finally Georgette heard her master say, "How about a thick slab of salami, Georgie?" Now salami was Georgette's absolutely favorite food and without thinking, she dashed out from under the couch.

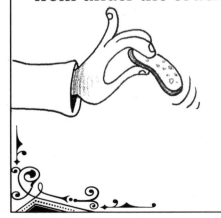

"Gotcha," Curious Georgette heard as she was firmly grasped. "Ha, ha, ha, we don't even have any salami," said the evil stepmother, as she stuffed Georgette into the oven—no, no, wait, that's the wrong fairy tale. What really happened is much worse. Curious Georgette was taken to the V-E-T and fixed, and spent the rest of her life listlessly watching TV in the family room since she really didn't feel like going out with the guys anymore.

This Is The Nook
Where Jack Slept

This is the nook where Jack slept.

This is the cat
That walked, pitter pat,
Right by the nook
Where Jack slept.

This is the smell
That dogs know so well
Which came from the cat
That walked, pitter pat,
Right by the nook
Where Jack slept.

This Is The Nook Where Jack Slept

This is the vase
With sides thin as gauze
That cost quite a lot
And stood by the spot
Right near the smell
That dogs know so well
Which came from the cat
That walked, pitter pat,
Right by the nook
Where Jack slept.

This Is The Nook Where Jack Slept

This is the mess
Its cause, you can guess:
When Jack sprang in haste
At the cat he would waste
And knocked down the vase
With sides thin as gauze
That cost quite a lot
And stood by the spot
Right near the smell
That dogs know so well
Which came from the cat
That walked, pitter pat,
Right by the nook
Where Jack slept.

The Little Red Dog

One day the Little Red Dog was walking along and she found a tobacco seed lying in the road. "Hmmmm," said the Little Red Dog, "this seed should be planted. Who will help me plant this seed?"
"Not I," said the Black Cat.
"Not I," said the Little Goldfish.
"Not I," said the Pet Canary.
"Then I will," said the Little Red Dog, and she did.

In time, the seed grew into a tall, healthy tobacco plant and the Little Red Dog thought it was time to pick it. "Who will help me pick the tobacco?" she asked.
"Not I," said the Black Cat.
"Not I," said the Little Goldfish.
"Not I," said the Pet Canary.
So the Little Red Dog picked the tobacco leaves herself. When the tobacco was picked, it was time to dry it, and again when the Little Red Dog asked her friends for help, all she got was a "Not I" from the lazy cat, goldfish and canary, though it was doubtful that the goldfish would have been much help anyway, since he tended to lie there and flop when out of the water. But at least he could have been nicer about it.

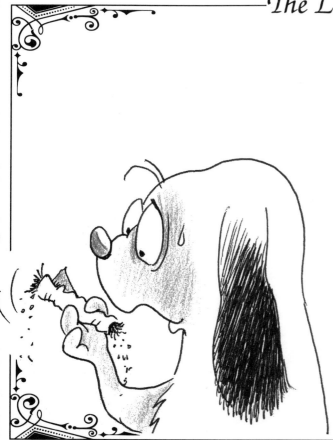

Anyhow, to make a long story short, when it came time to make the tobacco into cigarettes, the stupid lazy cat, goldfish and canary all gave their damn "Not I" again, and the Little Red Dog was left with the job of rolling the cigarettes, which is hard enough for a cowboy with ten fingers, but a really tough job for a dog that never was too good with her paws. But somehow she managed.

The Little Red Dog

When the cigarettes were rolled and ready, the Little Red Dog said, "Who will go to the corner bar with me to smoke these cigarettes?"
"Not I," said the Black Cat, "it's time for my run."
"Not I," said the Little Goldfish, "I have to lead the water aerobics class."
"Not I," said the Pet Canary, "I have to get some seeds and whole grain at the health food store."

So the Little Red Dog smoked all the cigarettes herself, developed terrible emphysema, high blood pressure and a cough you wouldn't believe, and was made to feel like a criminal whenever she lit up at a restaurant.

The Gnat In The Hat

There once was a Gnat
   Who was really a flea.
He lived on a dog,
   In a small colony.

This gnat was quite little,
   But was sort of tough,
And sported some teeth
   That chewed rather rough.

The gnat used to tickle,
  But mostly he'd bite.
The dog was not happy
  And put up a fight.

The dog tried to eat him
  And kill with his claw.
He wriggled and chased him,
  Until he was sore.

The flea hunkered down
  And caused such an itch,
The dog thought this creature
  Was really a bitch!

The Gnat In The Hat

He hated that Gnat;
    How he hated its guts.
The dog knew the insect
    Was driving him nuts.

Then one day his Master
    Came home with a box,
That contained a white powder
    To end this great pox.

This powder would choke them
    And make the Gnats ill.
The fleas all would hate it;
    With luck, it would kill.

*T*hey sprinkled flea powder
    All over their pet,
And although it was messy,
    The fleas were beset.

With coughing and sneezing
    And headaches galore,
They started to drop off
    And fell to the floor.

While most of them faltered,
    Still one flea stood pat.
This bug was determined,
    This Gnat in the Hat.

The Gnat held on bravely
    And when the air cleared,
He was all alone,
    And it felt kind of weird.

The dog knew the time
    To attack with new zest
Was just now upon him;
    He'd finish this pest.

He gnashed with his teeth,
    And he hit with his claw.
The Gnat just kept ducking
    And hid from the paw.

The Gnat became weary;
    He felt kind of weak.
"If I'm not welcome
    A new home I'll seek."

Not far lay a puss
    With a soft furry coat,
And the flea left right then,
    Without leaving a note.

So if you are plagued
    By a Gnat in a Hat,
The message is simple
    To get him to scat.

Go after him briskly
    With powder and claw.
If that doesn't kill him,
    He'll head for the door.

Puppy Picture Book

See the nice hydrant,
  So strong and so squat.
One squirt of wee wee
  Will not make it rot.

Sniffing around it,
  When I pass each day,
Tells me which playmates
  Have come by the way.

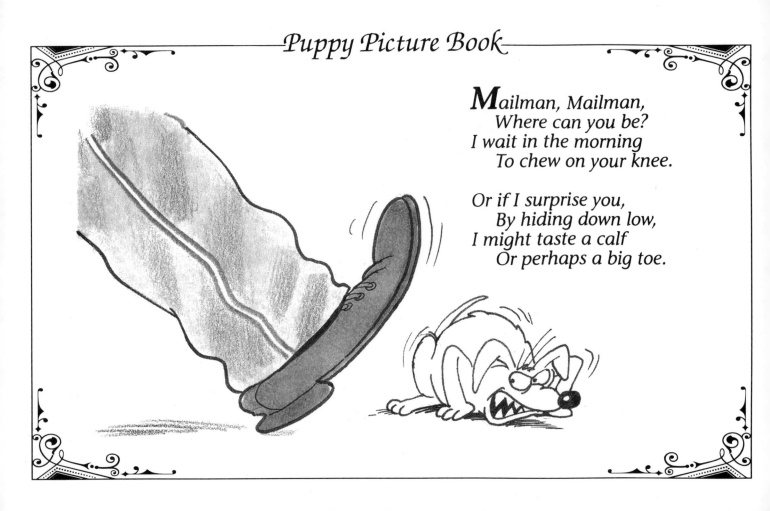

Mailman, Mailman,
　　Where can you be?
I wait in the morning
　　To chew on your knee.

Or if I surprise you,
　　By hiding down low,
I might taste a calf
　　Or perhaps a big toe.

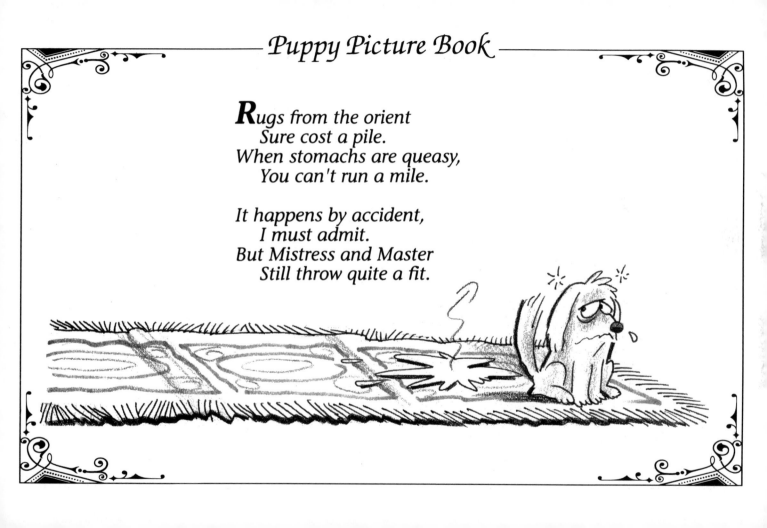

Rugs from the orient
　　Sure cost a pile.
When stomachs are queasy,
　　You can't run a mile.

It happens by accident,
　　I must admit.
But Mistress and Master
　　Still throw quite a fit.

Wait for the car
    To come right down the street.
Run at the tires;
    It's really a treat.

Watch how they swerve
    And go rushing away.
Here comes another;
    It's back to my play.

Goldipup And The Three Teddy Bears

Goldipup was a Golden Retriever who lived with a family in a white house in Shaker Heights. The little girl in the family had a beautiful pink and blue room upstairs with three teddy bears on her bed. Now Goldipup was a downstairs dog, and she was not allowed up to the bedrooms. But one day when the family was away, her curiosity got the better of her, and she crept upstairs.

You can imagine Goldi's surprise when she saw the three teddy bears. "What wonderful playmates they would make," and she jumped right up on the bed and started playing with the daddy teddy bear. Goldipup played with the bow around the teddy bear's neck, and she played with the bear's big nose so much, that eventually it fell off, but the daddy bear was too hard and too big for Goldi's taste.

Next, Goldi pounced on the momma teddy bear and clawed and scratched at it. She easily ripped open the momma bear and played for a while with all the stuffing. But the momma teddy bear was too soft and though she made quite a mess, it soon bored Goldipup. Then Goldipup found the baby teddy bear and, grabbing its head in her mouth, rolled around and around with it. This bear was just right and Goldi played with it all afternoon, managing to rip off the head and both arms, and to open quite a few seams in the crotch.

Goldipup And The Three Teddy Bears

When the little girl came home, she went to her room and found her daddy teddy bear minus his nose. Then she found her momma teddy bear or, I should say, the insides, spread all over the floor. The arms of her baby teddy bear were on the floor of her closet, but by this time she was so angry that she dumped her bowl of porridge over Goldipup. Goldi was frightened at first, but when she finally got back downstairs and started licking the porridge (which is really oatmeal in everything except fairy tales), found it tasted pretty good and spent the afternoon happily licking away.

Three Sick Ticks

Three sick ticks,
Three sick ticks,
See how they swell,
See how they swell.
They latched right onto a poodle's neck,
And clung quite tight tho' he scratched like heck,
These horrible things make your life a wreck.
Three sick ticks,
Three sick ticks.

Three Little Puppies

Three little puppies,
Owned by yuppies
With Persian rugs in the hall.

"Oh, Mother dear,
We sadly fear,
We've messed them one and all."

Three Little Puppies

"**Y**ou naughty mutts
You must be nuts
When nature's call you heed.

"Just go outdoors,
Not on my floors,
And do it with due speed."

The Alphabet Song

A, B, C, D, E, F, G,
How about a snack for me?
All of you are eating there,
I just get to sit and stare.
A, B, C, D, E, F, G,
Someone have some sympathy.

ack And The Beanstalk

Jack was an obedient little puppy who never had to be scolded and whose breath was sweet due to the dry dog food his mother fed him, which he really did not prefer to the expensive canned stuff. One day, his mother gave him a manufacturer's coupon for $.50 off a giant bag of doggy chow and sent him to the market.

On the way, Jack ran into a hip cat named Duke, who hung around the corner and was the local dealer. Duke inquired as to Jack's errand and with the help of a chain saw and a couple of Colombian buddies, talked Jack into trading his money and coupon for three little white pills.

Jack took one of the little white pills as he walked along, and by the time he arrived home, he was seeing beanstalks growing everywhere, including out of his ears and tail, not to mention some very bright psychedelic colors. Jack was so high, it was easy for him to climb one of the beanstalks. "Who knows," he thought, "there might be a golden goose at the top or maybe even canned dog food made out of Beef Pulp and Poultry Digest, whatever that is."

Jack climbed way up to the top of the beanstalk. It ended in a cloud, and Jack jumped off and almost got knocked over by Henney Penney who was running around screaming, "The sky is falling! The sky is falling! We must run and tell the king." At the time, it seemed the right thing to do, so Jack joined Henney Penney, Goosey Loosey, Cocky Locky and the rest of the idiots, and went off to find the king.

Jack And The Beanstalk

Along the way, they came upon a fierce giant who growled when he saw them, and said, "Fe Fi Fo Fum, I smell the blood of an Englishman," which Jack noticed didn't rhyme very good at all. The chickens, ducks and geese all got frightened and flapped off, but Jack wasn't concerned about the giant smelling his blood since he wasn't an Englishman, and he wasn't sure giants could smell blood since he had found people-type critters couldn't smell very well anyhow. By this time, the effects of the little white pill were wearing off, and Jack thought it might be a good idea to get away from all these nuts and go back to the kitchen where perhaps lunch was waiting.

Jack And The Beanstalk

Jack walked back to the beanstalk, which looked pretty high up indeed and rather scary to climb down. Way below, he could see his mother calling him, but dogs weren't supposed to climb trees and as his head started to clear, he realized that it was indeed a tree he was stuck in. He certainly didn't want the police or firefighters to come to find him, still a little spaced out and with those two other white pills in his pocket. So he stayed up in the tree until it got cold that evening and his mother opened a can of yummy "Mighty Dog." Then he jumped to the garage roof and down to the ground. When he came home, his mother cried and cried and grounded Jack for a month. The moral here, kiddies, is to never talk to strangers and to never ever take little white pills from them.

The Counting Song

1, 2, 3, 4, 5, 6, 7,
8, 9, 10, I count 11.
Surely they can't eat them all,
One small piece is bound to fall,
1, 2, 3, 4, 5, 6, 7,
If there is a God in heaven.

Jack And Jill

Jack and Jill were outside dogs, and one day they went up the hill. They didn't go up the hill for water or anything stupid like that. Water you get from a faucet or at least from a hose around a barn. They went up the hill to get a little privacy 'cause Jill was in heat and she wanted some action in the worst way.

Jack And Jill

When Jack and Jill got up the hill, they found a cozy spot and did "you know what" — after which Jill wanted to lay around and snuggle, but Jack said he was hungry and went looking for a pizza. Jack seldom felt romantic after sex.

A few weeks later when Jill was starting "to show," the farmer's wife got so angry, she ran after her with a carving knife and threatened to cut off her tail, but that's another story. With all the hubbub that Jill's pregnancy was causing (she had broken up with Jack by this point and had decided to move in with a friend and try her hand at being a single parent), the time just flew by and before long, the puppies were cuddling in the birthing box.

Jack, meanwhile, had taken up with an aerobics instructor from his club. When Jill ran into them one day at the mall and saw the floozie swishing her tight little body around, she lost her temper, whacked Jack with a can of Spaghetti-O's and broke his crown.

Little Pup Blue

Little Pup Blue,
   Come jump and growl.
A suspicious person
   Is on the prowl.

It's time to bark
   And chase this louse,
Before he comes
   Into the house.

But Master calls you
   Off with grief,
It is his Mom
   And not a thief.

ary Had A Puppy Dog

Mary had a puppy dog,
    Its coat was white as snow,
And everywhere that Mary went
    The dog was sure to go.

When Mary and her beau would smooch,
    Upon the parlor floor,
Her pup would sit and watch them both
    'Til thrown out the door.

Monday's Pup

Monday's pup is fair of face.
Tuesday's dog just loves to chase.
Wednesday's on his leash will tow.
Thursday's runs for balls you throw.
Friday's sometimes makes a mess.
Saturday's eats to excess.
But pups born on the Sabbath Day,
Will always find a tree to spray.